DIESELS IN THE
WEST MIDLANDS

Plate 1: Birmingham, at the heart of the West Midlands, has been dubbed 'The Motor City'. Viewed from beneath 'Spaghetti Junction' and running alongside the elevated section of the A38(M), the diverted 'Sundays only' 08.51 Leeds to Plymouth HST approaches Aston.
4th December 1983   *Geoff Dowling*

Plate 2: Birmingham Skyline.

DIESELS

in the

WEST MIDLANDS

Geoff Dowling and John Whitehouse

Oxford Publishing Company

Typesetting by:
Aquarius Typesetting Services, New Milton, Hants.

Printed in Great Britain by:
Biddles Ltd., Guildford, Surrey.

Published by:
Oxford Publishing Co.
Link House
West Street
POOLE, Dorset

Plate 3: The old order at Kingswinford Junction survives into the 1980s as Class 25 No. 25032 heads a local trip working towards Bescot.

12th December 1983   *Geoff Dowling*

Introduction

The West Midlands comprises the counties of Warwickshire, Worcester and much of Staffordshire and Shropshire. As well as the birthplace of the Industrial Revolution at Coalbrookdale the area includes such historical centres as Shrewsbury, Worcester, Lichfield and Stratford-upon-Avon. Although the Midlands is usually associated with the industrialised landscape of Birmingham and the Black Country, much of the surrounding countryside is agricultural and contains some areas of quite outstanding natural beauty.

Railways came to the Midlands in the first half of the nineteenth century, rapidly displacing the extensive canal system, but often closely following the waterways for many miles. The rail network spread to connect and serve the major centres of population, and to carry the raw materials and manufactured goods associated with the industrial areas of Birmingham, the Black Country and the Potteries. At the 1923 Grouping, the smaller railway companies were amalgamated into the LMS and GWR, leaving the Midlands with a comprehensive rail system which remains largely extant today.

Birmingham (New Street) Station is situated at the very centre of the British Rail network and a number of important cross-country routes, principally from East Anglia and Wales, feed traffic to the major arterial routes that pass through Birmingham. Recent developments of the motorway system mean increasing competition from road transport; a situation parallel to that of 150 years ago between railways and waterways.

In preparing this album we have tried to capture the atmosphere of the West Midlands by showing current operations and also some of the changes that have occurred over the last twenty five years. We have attempted to give more space to the less well-known locations, and feature trains whose importance both to the region and its railways are often overlooked.

In conclusion, we would like to thank the staff of British Rail for their co-operation during many hours of photography, Michael Mensing for his willing assistance with archive material, and Jean Dowling for drawing the maps.

John Whitehouse and Geoff Dowling

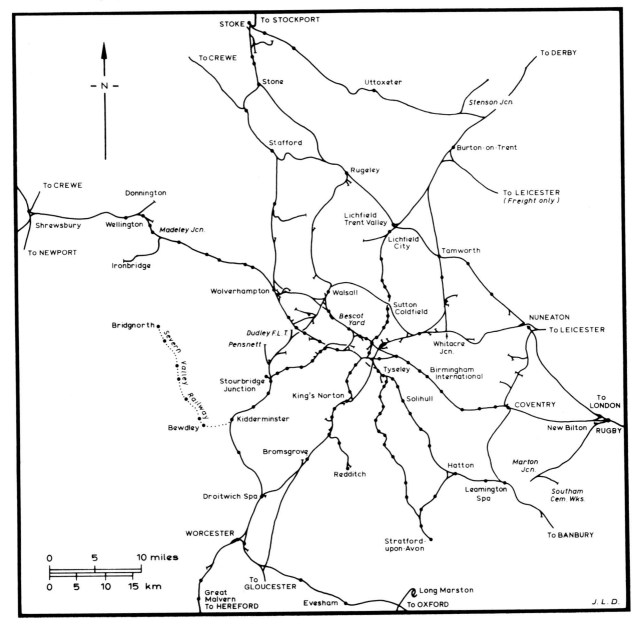

Plate 4 (above): The ramparts of Shrewsbury Castle provide an excellent platform from which to watch railway operations. This view, looking towards Abbey Foregate, illustrates the variety of motive power to be seen. Class 33 No. 33008 *Eastleigh* departs with the 10.00 Crewe to Cardiff, working whilst Class 25s Nos. 25209 and 25242 prepare to follow with the 07.40 Euston to Aberystwyth train.

11th September 1982　　　　　　　*Geoff Dowling*

Plate 6 (right): Class 25 No. 25051 shunts Sutton Bridge permanent way yard on 18th May 1985. Note the mixture of upper and lower quadrant semaphore signals in evidence.

　　　　　　　　　　　　　　　Geoff Dowling

Plate 5 (above): Access to Abbey Yard is gained via the now truncated Severn Valley route, and Class 08 No. 08686 is seen at the oil terminal with the morning trip working. Note the locally-manufactured crane with wooden jib.
26th February 1985   *Geoff Dowling*

Plate 7 (above): The Crewe test train, which usually runs to Church Stretton, has, since steam days, brought a tremendous variety of locomotives to Shrewsbury. 'ScotRail' Class 47 No. 47714, now named *Grampian Region*, heads back to Crewe with the test train on 26th February 1985.

Geoff Dowling

Plate 8 (below): Class 33 No. 33019 approaches Sutton Bridge Junction with the 07.45 Cardiff to Manchester train on a crisp February morning in 1985. The signals protect the Junction of the Cambrian line.

Geoff Dowling

Plate 9: On the approach to Hookagate, Class 25s Nos. 25205 and 25218 strain to accelerate the 10.10 Euston to Aberystwyth train away from Shrewsbury on 11th August 1984.

Geoff Dowling

Plate 10: Less than a year later, and Class 37s have replaced the unreliable Class 25s; Nos. 37186 and 37124 head the 07.30 Euston to Aberystwyth working away from Sutton Bridge Junction on 18th May 1985.

Geoff Dowling

Plate 11: From its dominant position, All Saints Church overlooks Wellington Station, whilst Class 47 No. 47209 heads east with the Waterston to Albion tanks on 16th February 1985.

Geoff Dowling

Plate 12: A military special brings Class 20s Nos. 20093 and 20019 to the truncated Wellington to Stafford branch line. The line closed in 1966 and the short branch is retained to serve Donnington Army Depot.
16th February 1985   *Geoff Dowling*

Plate 13: Class 25s Nos. 25268 and 25313 head the 10.10 Euston to Aberystwyth train into Wellington, passing the unusual bracket signal to the east of the station.
18th August 1984   John Whitehouse

Plate 14: Returning from Donnington Army Depot, Class 31 No. 31178 heads the daily freight from Bescot at Trench Crossing.
2nd July 1985   Geoff Dowling

Plate 15: Before the withdrawal of the passenger service, Class 122 railcar No. 55012 is pictured having just crossed Coalbrookdale Viaduct whilst operating the 17.50 Wellington to Much Wenlock service on 9th June 1962. The clock tower is part of the Coalbrookdale Company premises, where also can be found Abraham Darby's original blast furnaces. This, indeed, is the cradle of the Industrial Revolution.

Michael Mensing

Plate 16: The line now only carries coal and oil to Buildwas Power-Station and was utilised by several merry-go-round trains daily. Unfortunately much traffic was lost during the 1984/85 miners' strike. Class 20s with slow speed control have recently been introduced, and on an early July day in 1985 Nos. 20060 and 20160 climb from Ironbridge Gorge with a return working to Trentham. *2nd July 1985*

Geoff Dowling

Plate 17: Class 47 No. 47199 crosses Coalbrookdale Viaduct with a returning merry-go-round trip to Littleton Colliery on 2nd July 1985.

Geoff Dowling

Plate 18: A short distance upstream from Ironbridge, it is appropriate that the branch crosses the River Severn by the Albert Edward Bridge, a single 200ft. span iron bridge, built in 1862. Note the similarity to the more famous Victoria Bridge at Arley on the Severn Valley Railway. Class 58 No. 58001 provides the motive power of the 1980s, leading a loaded merry-go-round train into Buildwas Power-Station.
2nd July 1985

Geoff Dowling

Plate 19 (top left): A Class 47 locomotive, No. 47625 *City of Truro,* passes the now-closed New Hadley Halt with the 11.40 Euston to Shrewsbury train on 27th February 1985.

Geoff Dowling

Plate 20 (bottom left): The Ironbridge branch joins the main Shrewsbury to Wolverhampton line at Madeley Junction, Telford. Class 47 No. 47437 speeds past at the head of the 16.40 Shrewsbury to Euston working on 6th August 1983.

Geoff Dowling

Plate 21 (right): The station at Cosford serves RAF Cosford and the Indoor Athletics track, whilst the hangars behind the signal box house an interesting Aircraft Museum. A Class 120 diesel multiple unit, with car No. 50739 leading, approaches with the 10.24 local train from Shrewsbury to Wolverhampton. Note the recently converted upper quadrant semaphores on ex-GWR signal posts.
26th June 1982   *Geoff Dowling*

Plate 22 (below): The summer-dated 10.07 Aberystwyth to Euston working approaches Shifnal Station on 26th June 1982 with the then usual pair of Class 25s, No. 25085 leading.

Geoff Dowling

Plate 23 (above): Returning to London from a visit to Newtown, a 'Mid-Wales Development Charter' comprising the VSOE Pullmans brings Class 33 No. 33056 *The Burma Star* to the outskirts of Cosford on 7th July 1984.

Geoff Dowling

Plate 24 (below): More usual power, on 30th June 1984, as Class 47 No. 47558 *Mayflower* races non-stop through the charming ex-GWR station of Albrighton, whilst hauling the 09.40 Shrewsbury to Euston express.

Geoff Dowling

Plate 25: Oxley Carriage Sidings are to the left of the viaduct that carries the line over the Staffordshire and Worcestershire Canal. Having replaced an electric locomotive at Wolverhampton, Class 47 No. 47603 accelerates the 11.40 ex-Euston express towards its final destination of Shrewsbury. Stafford Road viaduct is visible in the background.
16th June 1984   Geoff Dowling

Plate 26: Until electrification, the Shrewsbury line ran into Wolverhampton (Low Level) Station, which finally closed in 1972. Still remarkably intact, it is now hardly used, except for parcels traffic. In June 1984, withdrawn Class 25 No. 25067 was dumped here after use as a depot exhibit.
John Whitehouse

Plate 27: Diverted to the ex-GWR route via Wolverhampton (Low Level), Class 40 No. D329 approaches Cannock Road Junction with the 08.30 Bangor to Birmingham train. This through route from Busbury Junction closed in 1968, but a spur (left) was retained for merry-go-round traffic to the Ironbridge branch. To avoid running round, this spur was replaced by the Oxley East Chord in 1983. Southern Region coaches are also seen in this view.

26th June 1966   *Michael Mensing*

Plate 28: Penkridge is the only station between Wolverhampton and Stafford, and is used solely by local services. On 17th August 1985, the 12.10 Liverpool to Plymouth HST service speeds through the station.

John Whitehouse

Plate 29: Wolverhampton (High Level) Station today, with HST power car No. 43191 leading the 12.10 Liverpool to Plymouth IC125 service into the station, in September 1985. Note that the power car is in the old-style livery whilst the stock is in the new executive colours. HSTs were introduced on to this route in May 1984 to improve through journey times and avoid a locomotive change at Birmingham (New Street).

Geoff Dowling

Plate 30 (left): To the north of Wolverhampton, the Stour Valley and Grand Junction lines meet at Bushbury Junction. On 10th August 1985 the 05.25 Plymouth to Liverpool HST curves through the junction with power car No. 43022 leading.

John Whitehouse

Plate 31 (below): Class 47 No. 47449 approaches Wolverhampton North Junction with the 13.52 Liverpool to Portsmouth train on 7th September 1985. The lines in the foreground go to Oxley and Shrewsbury. Stafford Road Viaduct is seen beyond the locomotive.

Ivor Ford

Plate 32 (above right): Turning around from the view in *Plate 31*, No. 43011 leads the 11.10 Paignton to Manchester working away from Wolverhampton. Note the well-maintained flight of locks which leads to a renovated town centre marina.

7th September 1985   *Geoff Dowling*

WOLVERHAMPTON NORTH JUNCTION

Plate 33 (below): To the south of Wolverhampton, the first station on the Stour Valley route is Coseley, where Class 47/3 No. 47333 strains against the gradient with the 06.33 Poole to Manchester service on 24th August 1985.

John Whitehouse

Plate 34 (above): The 1985 Crewe remodelling resulted in North Wales services changing locomotives at Stafford. On 29th June 1985, Class 47 No. 47492 makes an enthusiastic start after taking over the 14.00 Euston to Holyhead train from electric traction.

Geoff Dowling

Plate 35 (below): The 06.14 Bristol to Manchester IC125 service approaches the junction with the Stoke to Colwich line at Stone. The HST has travelled via Norton Bridge on the West Coast Main Line, from Stafford. Note the attractive North Staffordshire Railway station building situated within the junction.
8th June 1985   *Geoff Dowling*

Plate 36: A pre-electrification scene at Stafford. Class 40 No. D267 attracts attention as it arrives with the 13.05 Llandudno to Euston working on 4th March 1961. This canopy is all that was left of the old station which was to be rebuilt as part of the West Coast Electrification Scheme. At this time, however, the work had been halted whilst the whole concept was reappraised.

Michael Mensing

Plate 37: Happily the scheme was completed, and this 1985 view shows the modern Stafford Station and a heavy Bangor to Northampton parcels service hauled by Class 25 No. 25211. Compare the view with that in *Plate 36*.
29th June 1985

Geoff Dowling

Plate 38: Having lost its passenger service under the Beeching axe, Walsall to Rugeley (Trent Valley) remains open for freight and frequent Sunday passenger diversions. On 1st April 1984, Class 40 No. 40118 approaches Marquis's Drive level crossing on Cannock Chase, hauling the diverted 08.25 Liverpool to Paddington service.

Geoff Dowling

Plate 39: A local trip working from Lea Hall to Mid-Cannock utilises Class 45 power in the shape of No. 45068, seen coasting down easy gradients at Hednesford. The old platforms can be seen to the right of the rear of the train.
9th March 1984   Geoff Dowling

Plate 40: Local National Coal Board expansion has brought extra traffic to the line, serving primarily Essington Wood washing plant, Mid-Cannock Colliery and Lea Hall Power-Station, although most of the traffic for the latter is received via the Trent Valley route. Merry-go-round empties from Lea Hall pass Hednesford on 9th March 1984 behind Class 56 No. 56061.
Geoff Dowling

Plate 41: Framed in the remains of the steam shed at Stafford, Class 47 No. 47528 awaits its next duty on 29th June 1985.

Geoff Dowling

Plate 42: At Rugeley, the Trent Valley line is quadruple track to accommodate Colwich Junction, some two miles to the west. A northbound engineer's train carrying continuous welded rail, with Class 31 No. 31126 in charge, hurries by on 18th April 1985.

John Whitehouse

Plate 43: Freight activity at Rugeley, some ten years earlier. A northbound freightliner, hauled by Class 87 No. 87004 (now named *Britannia*) meets Class 47 No. 47329, which has just run round its train of merry-go-round hoppers, and will shortly proceed to Rugeley Power-Station.
11th June 1975

Geoff Dowling

Plate 44: Rugeley (Trent Valley) Station in January 1960, as an afternoon service to Birmingham (via Walsall) awaits departure. All that remains today is a ubiquitous bus shelter. Lea Hall Power-Station can be seen in the top left-hand corner.
Michael Mensing

Plate 45: Locally, hopes are high that a passenger service will return to the Walsall route, as the northern end has seen considerable housing developments over the years. Hopefully, this pastoral scene, with Class 47 No. 47441 in charge of the 09.55 Gatwick to Manchester Sunday working at Slitting Mill near Rugeley, will become an everyday sight in the future.
1st April 1984   *Geoff Dowling*

Plate 46: Another Sunday diversion brings Class 47 No. 47403 *The Geordie* on to the Trent Valley line at Rugeley with the 13.05 Birmingham to Liverpool service in late March 1984.

Geoff Dowling

Plate 47: Whilst most of the West Coast Main Line is signalled from power boxes, the Trent Valley line has retained some signal boxes. Passing Tamworth with a 'down' ballast train, Class 25 No. 25315 will have to await a path north until there is a lull in the high-speed electrically-hauled traffic.
31st August 1985
Geoff Dowling

Plate 48 (above): Class 40 No. D325 passes Abbey Junction signal box at Nuneaton with the up 'Royal Scot'. A steam hauled freight awaits access to the Trent Valley from the Market Bosworth line (now closed).

Michael Mensing

Plate 49 (below): A Ford Company train from Halewood to Dagenham is looped at Lichfield (Trent Valley) to allow an express to overtake. Running very late, it is probable that a failure of the booked electric locomotive has resulted in the unusual appearance of a Class 47 locomotive, No. 47264, at the head of the train.

6th September 1977   *John Whitehouse*

Plate 50 (above): Railtour duty presents a rare opportunity for a pair of Class 25s to show their paces along the Trent Valley. Speeding through Polesworth Station, Nos. 25034 and 25044 head for Stafford with 'The North Midlander' railtour of 23rd February 1985.

John Whitehouse

Plate 51 (below): Providing a welcome relief from the procession of West Coast expresses, Class 31 No. 31413 has just threaded the junction off the Leicester line, and eases the 07.40 Norwich to Birmingham train into Nuneaton Station.
9th March 1985   *John Whitehouse*

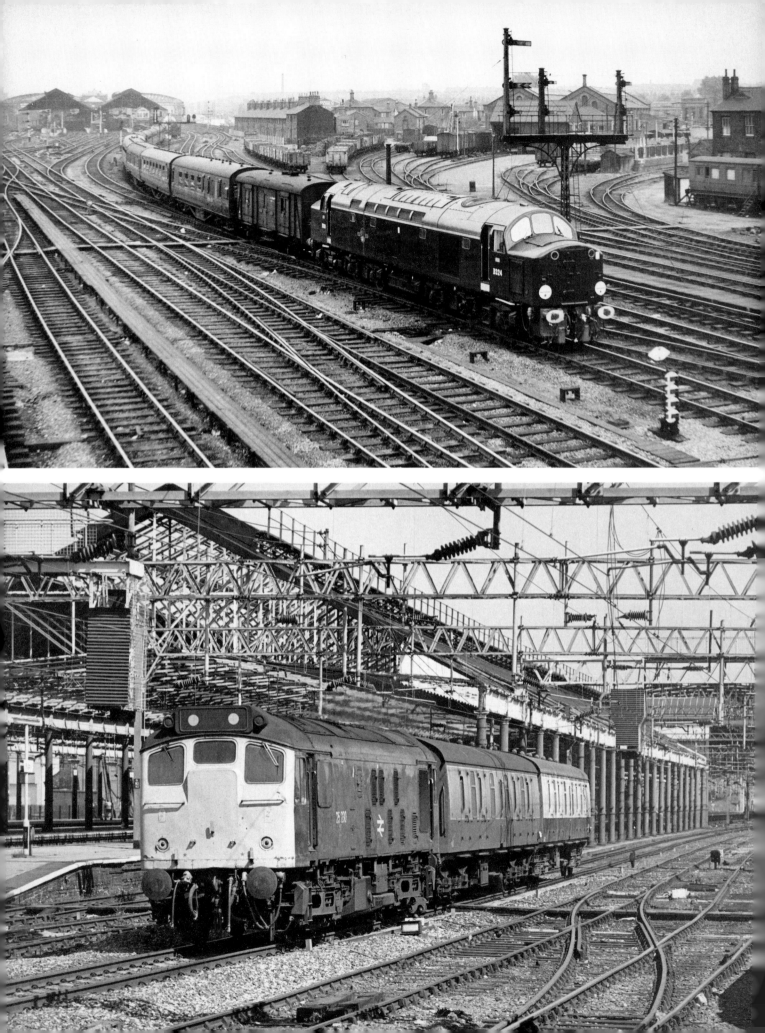

Plate 54 (above): The line to Leamington Spa closed to passengers in 1959, and was truncated at Marton Junction in 1966. Traffic, albeit sparse, still uses the route to Southam Cement Works, whilst daily trip workings, here with Class 08 shunter No. 08807 in charge, operate to New Bilton (Rugby Cement). Note the unusual semaphore signal.
22nd August 1985   Geoff Dowling

Plate 55 (right): Some nineteen years earlier than the view seen in Plate 54, a freight, hauled by Class 24 No. D5137, taking coal to Southam (via Marton Junction), passes the same location.
21st July
1966   Michael Mensing

Plate 52 (above left): Although electrification has not changed the station too much, panoramic views such as this are no longer possible at Rugby. Class 40 No. D324 is at the head of the 13.10 Euston to Glasgow express on 22nd July 1961. The old Great Central viaduct is visible behind the station.

Michael Mensing

Plate 53 (left): Beneath a mass of catenary, Class 25 No. 25230 takes the through line at Rugby at the head of a Bletchley to Birmingham (Curzon Street) parcels working.
30th May 1985   Geoff Dowling

Plate 56: Trundling through Fenton, one of the five towns forming 'The Potteries' is a Class 120 diesel multiple unit with the 09.20 Crewe to Nottingham service. Note the pottery and bottle kiln behind the train.
8th June 1985   Geoff Dowling

Plate 57: The Stoke to Derby line is primarily the preserve of diesel multiple units, but summer Saturdays saw locomotive haulage on the Nottingham to Llandudno service. On 26th June 1982, Class 47 No. 47329 heads the return working into Uttoxeter. Alas, this service has since been diagrammed for a diesel multiple unit.

Geoff Dowling

Plate 58 (above): A diesel multiple unit failure resulted in a Class 25, No. 25182, being called upon to provide a replacement service, to the obvious glee of at least one traveller. The train passing Foley Crossing, Longton on 29th June 1984 is the 13.20 Derby to Crewe.

Geoff Dowling

Plate 59 (below): A scene to linger on and enjoy is this charcteristic view on the ex-North Staffordshire route, as a Class 118 unit, forming the 14.20 Crewe to Cleethorpes service, meanders through Scropton, with its impressive church. A military line used to diverge at this point.
31st August 1984 *Geoff Dowling*

Plate 60 (above): A trip movement of freightliner flats to Beeston Freightliner Terminal brings Class 25 No. 25211 to Uttoxeter on 1st October 1985.

Geoff Dowling

Plate 61 (left): A Class 120 unit heads the 13.20 Crewe to Lincoln service through Scropton Crossing on 31st August 1984. Note the Metropolitan-Cammell trailer inserted between the two driving cars.

Geoff Dowling

Plate 62 (above right): 'The Midland Executive' railtour passes Tutbury Yard with Class 40 No. 40122 (D200) in charge. The scene, here recorded on 2nd June 1984, has since been drastically altered by rationalisation.

Geoff Dowling

Plate 63 (below right): Class 31 No. 31169 heads a southbound freight through Stenson Junction on 12th May 1976. The tracks on the right lead to Willington Power-Station, whilst the branch in the right background goes to Long Eaton and Toton.

Geoff Dowling

Plate 64 (above): Heading south along the Midland main line from Burton-upon-Trent are Class 31 locomotives, Nos. 31232 and 31294, with a block cement train. They are passing the site of Barton and Walton Station; the goods shed survives, but nothing remains of the station which closed in 1958. *6th July 1985*   *Geoff Dowling*

Plate 65 (below): The summer-dated 09.07 Burton-upon-Trent to Skegness working has been hauled by Class 20 locomotives for several years, and on 31st May 1984 Nos. 20227 and 20216 head the train past Wetmore Sidings. The flyover carried the branch from Burton (Horninglow) to Tutbury, which closed in 1966.

Geoff Dowling

Plate 66 (above): Burton-upon-Trent is famed for brewing and the Ind Coope Brewery dominates the skyline as Class 45/1 No. 45143 *5th Royal Inniskilling Dragoon Guards* restarts the 08.29 Leeds to Cardiff train. Note the wide island platform.
9th April 1985   *Geoff Dowling*

Plate 67 (below): Crossing the River Trent on Wychnor Junction viaduct, the 09.10 Paignton to Newcastle train is hauled by Class 31 locomotives Nos. 31234 and 31275. At this point the line from Walsall and Lichfield joins the Midland main line.
6th July 1985   *Geoff Dowling*

Plate 68 (above): Climbing the spur from the Trent Valley, Class 58 No. 58003 hauls an empty merry-go-round working from Rugeley past Lichfield (Trent Valley) Junction on 19th April 1985. The level crossing closed some months earlier.

John Whitehouse

Plate 69 (below): Having travelled via the freight only line from Walsall, Class 45/0 No. 45060 *Sherwood Forester* approaches Lichfield City with a Wolverhampton to Wadsley Bridge 'Footex' on 11th April 1981.

Geoff Dowling

Plate 70: Sutton Coldfield signal box closed in October 1980 when control of the area passed to Four Oaks. With the resignalling work well in hand, a Class 116 diesel multiple unit, with a Longbridge to Four Oaks service, passes with caution.
5th October 1980   *John Whitehouse*

Plate 71: Class 47 No. 47297 shunts the thrice-weekly train of oil from Immingham at Anglesey Sidings, Brownhills, situated on the Lichfield to Walsall line. The line is now closed south of this point.
9th May 1984   *John Whitehouse*

Plate 72: The 'Sutton Park' route forms an important freight connection from the ex-Midland line near Water Orton to Bescot, via Walsall. An interesting empty coaching stock working during the summer of 1981, from Worcester to Birmingham (New Street), regularly produced Class 50s, with No. 50005 *Collingwood* providing the power on 1st August. Note the remains of Sutton Park Station on the right.

Ivor Ford

Plate 73: There still remains a large post office parcels depot at Sutton Park, part of which occupies the old goods shed. Completing this scene, on 12th September 1981, is Class 31 No. 31324, running light from Bescot.

Robin Banks

Plate 74: In October 1963 a diesel multiple unit, forming the 13.46 Walsall to Birmingham (New Street) service, via Penns, leaves Sutton Park Station. The passenger service was withdrawn in January 1965.

Michael Mensing

Plate 75: At Ryecroft Junction, Class 56 No. 56087 takes the Sutton Park line with the 19.45 Bescot to Doncaster Speedlink working on 15th July 1984.

Geoff Dowling

Plate 76: Diverted via Lichfield, Class 45/0 No. 45041 *Royal Tank Regiment* speeds through Wylde Green whilst heading the 08.00 (Sunday) Bristol to Newcastle service on 22nd June 1981.

John Whitehouse

Plate 77: The Cross-City route has been used for evaluating the new types of diesel multiple unit, and on 16th April 1985 it was the turn of the Metro-Cammell Class 151 unit, seen here pausing at Butlers Lane.

John Whitehouse

Plate 78: A more traditional scene, with Class 116 units passing to the south of Lichfield on Cross-City line services. The three spires of Lichfield Cathedral dominate the horizon.
16th April 1985   *John Whitehouse*

Plate 79: Sunday engineering work brings Class 45/0 No. 45009 to Gravelly Hill with a spoiled ballast train. Note the signal interlocked detonator placer.
31st March 1985   *Geoff Dowling*

Plates 80 & 81: Contrasting scenes at Whitacre Junction. In May 1963 a Leicester to Birmingham diesel miltiple unit restarts from the station. The junction can be clearly seen beyond the footbridge. Twenty years later *(below)*, the station, which closed in 1968, has been obliterated, although the track layout is the same. Class 20s Nos. 20155 and 20165 ease off the loop with an engineering train.

*Michael Mensing
and Geoff Dowling*

Plate 82: The Sunday diversions of Euston trains via Nuneaton have a reputation for producing interesting motive power. The 09.57 Wolverhampton to Euston on 31st March 1985 was no exception, being hauled by Class 58 No. 58009 through Whitacre.

John Whitehouse

Plate 83: At Water Orton, where the Tamworth and Nuneaton lines diverge, Class 46 No. 46027 rounds the curve past the disused signal box with the 14.39 Leeds to Plymouth service on 22nd July 1978.

Geoff Dowling

Plate 84 (above): Passing Hams Hall Power-Station at Lea Marston, a clean Class 47, No. 47575, catches the afternoon sun on 25th May 1985 whilst hauling the 13.55 Cardiff to Hull working.

Geoff Dowling

Plate 85 (top right): On test from Derby, HST power cars Nos. 43060 and 43061 return north after a run to Saltley.
19th January 1985

Geoff Dowling

Plate 86 (bottom right): Class 31 No. 31282 is pictured with the 13.24 Hull to Brighton train at Kingsbury on 3rd June 1985. Note the branch to Birch Coppice Colliery leaving the main line to the right.

Geoff Dowling

Plate 87: Daw Mill Colliery dominates this view as Class 31 No. 31438 passes with the 16.48 'Sundays only' Birmingham to Norwich service.
22nd April 1984 *Geoff Dowling*

Plate 88: A Sunday diversion passes Abbey Junction signal box, with Class 47 No. 47318 hauling Class 87 No. 87025 *Borderer* at the head of the 09.57 Wolverhampton to Euston service. The train will revert to electric traction at Nuneaton.
22nd April 1979 *Geoff Dowling*

Plate 89 (above): The route from Nuneaton to Coventry is normally for freight only, but a mystery excursion brought Class 47 No. 47439 to the line on 11th April 1982. The location is Hawkesbury Lane, on the outskirts of Coventry.

Geoff Dowling

Plate 90 (below): The exhaust is testimony to the effort that Class 58 No. 58023 is making to get a Keresley to Didcot merry-go-round train on the move, at Three Spires Junction, Coventry. *22nd August 1985*

Geoff Dowling

Plate 91: Passing Berkswell at the head of the 12.20 Lawley Street to Southampton Freightliner is Class 56 No. 56062. In the foreground is the truncated remains of the line to Kenilworth Junction.
9th April 1983

Geoff Dowling

Plate 92: Another Lawley Street to Southampton Freightliner, this time with Class 31 No. 31101 leaving Beechwood Tunnel, between Berkswell and Tile Hill.
27th July 1985

Ivor Ford

Plate 93: An appreciative crowd await Class 50 No. 50032 *Courageous* to draw to a halt with the 05.50 Paddington to Manchester train at Coventry on 30th April 1983. The locomotive will work through to Birmingham (New Street).

Geoff Dowling

Plate 94: Class 50 No. 50035 *Ark Royal* leads the 14.38 Birmingham to Paddington working from Coventry on 1st September 1981. The Leamington line was reopened to passenger traffic in the late 1970s to maximise the potential of the National Exhibition Centre.

Geoff Dowling

Plate 95 (left): A Metro-Cammell diesel multiple unit is pictured heading for Coventry, with a train from Leamington Spa (Avenue), and is passing Kenilworth Junction signal box. The Berkswell line passes behind the signal box.
25th June 1964   *Michael Mensing*

Plate 96 (below): The River Leam Weir in Leamington forms an attractive setting as Class 47 No. 47434 passes with the 12.54 Brighton to Manchester service on 30th March 1985.
Geoff Dowling

Plate 97 (above):   Kenilworth Junction, today, with Class 47 No. 47408 *Finsbury Park* hauling the 09.50 Birmingham to Portsmouth service. The left-hand arch once accommodated the Berkswell line, and a proposed mining scheme may see this section reopened.
6th May 1985   *Geoff Dowling*

Plate 98 (below): Kenilworth Station, which closed in 1965, remained virtually intact until eventual demolition in 1984. On 31st August 1981, Class 50 No. 50021 *Rodney* disturbs the peace with the 14.38 Birmingham to Paddington working.

Geoff Dowling

Plate 99: Taking the centre road at Leamington Spa is Class 33 No. 33042 with the 09.20 Lawley Street to Southampton (Millbrook) Freightliner working.
18th February 1984   *Geoff Dowling*

Plate 100: Easing out of the station and on to the viaduct, which carries the railway from Leamington, is the 09.20 Manchester to Poole express with Class 31 No. 31417 in command.
18th February 1984   *Geoff Dowling*

Plate 101: Leamington Spa (Avenue) Station, which closed in 1965 was the terminus for trains to Nuneaton and Rugby. On 24th June 1961, a Nuneaton-bound diesel multiple unit reverses into the westbound platform.
Michael Mensing

Plate 102: Class 47 No. 47558 *Mayflower* climbs away from Leamington Spa with the 12.50 Birmingham to Poole train on 27th July 1985.
Geoff Dowling

Plate 103 (left): The ex-GWR station nameboard echoes the former status of Bearley Junction, which now consists of an overgrown platform and bus shelter. Class 122 railcar No. 55004 leaves with the 10.48 Leamington to Stratford-upon-Avon service on 27th February 1982.

Geoff Dowling

Plate 105 (right): Class 52 No. 1052 *Western Viceroy* was an unusual visitor to Stratford-upon-Avon in March 1975, en route from Plymouth to Derby with an enthusiasts' special.

John Whitehouse

Plate 104 (below): Pausing at Wilmcote, a station notable for its classic GWR design, is a Class 116 diesel multiple unit with car No. 50116 leading, forming the 12.10 Birmingham (Moor Street) to Stratford-upon-Avon service.
19th June 1982   *Geoff Dowling*

Plate 106 (below): Stratford-upon-Avon on 13th July 1985. On the left, No. 53082 has arrived leading the 13.10 from Birmingham (Moor Street) whilst No. 53818 is the rear car of the 14.10 departure to Leamington Spa.

Geoff Dowling

Plate 107: If BR's proposals are accepted, Henley in Arden will become the southern terminus of the North Warwicks line. The usual Class 116 approaches on 23rd October 1982 with the 14.10 Birmingham (Moor Street) to Stratford-upon-Avon service.

Geoff Dowling

Plate 108: A Class 116 diesel multiple unit, with car No. 53890 leading, arrives at Danzey with the 11.20 Stratford-upon-Avon to Birmingham (Moor Street) working on 13th July 1985.

Geoff Dowling

Plate 109 (above): A cold night at Shirley, on 15th January 1985, as a Class 101 unit, encrusted with snow, prepares to reverse after forming the 19.40 ex-Birmingham (Moor Street) working.

Geoff Dowling

Plate 110 (below): In charge of a Severn Tunnel Junction-bound freight, Class 45/0 No. 45061 is a welcome change from the diet of diesel multiple units at Yardley Wood on 30th June 1976.

Geoff Dowling

Plate 111: The Birmingham to Stratford-upon-Avon services cross at Wood End and, on 13th July 1985, unit No. 53124 leads the 10.20 from Stratford whilst a similar Class 116 unit forms the 10.10 working from Birmingham (Moor Street).

Geoff Dowling

Plate 112: Hall Green signal box closed in August 1984, and all traces of the building have now gone. Shortly before closure, Class 47 No. 47475 passes with a return school charter from Yardley Wood on 30th June 1984.

Geoff Dowling

Plate 113: On 15th January 1984, Birmingham City Centre dominates the horizon, as Class 47 No. 47557 approaches Small Heath with the 08.25 Liverpool to Paddington working.

Geoff Dowling

Plate 114: A Sunday engineering diversion brought an HST to Tyseley on 10th February 1985. Power car No. 43031 leads the 07.45 Bristol to Newcastle (Sundays only working). The North Warwickshire line junction is seen to the right.

Geoff Dowling

Plate 115: To the north of Leamington, the ex-GWR main line has lost most of its expresses, but still carries a considerable amount of freight, mainly coal trains to Didcot Power-Station. Class 58 locomotive, No. 58011, passes Bentley Heath crossing with a loaded southbound merry-go-round train on a late August evening in 1985.
Geoff Dowling

Plate 116: On 2nd May 1965, Class 47 No. D1733, in experimental blue livery, approaches Knowle & Dorridge on the slow line with the 15.20 Wolverhampton (Low Level) to Paddington service. Note the variety of upper and lower quadrant signals evident at this time.

Michael Mensing

Plate 117: In their latter years, Class 52 diesel hydraulics were frequent visitors to Birmingham from Paddington. The 09.05 from Paddington was booked for 'Western' haulage, and on 26th April 1975 No. D1051 *Western Ambassador* had charge of the train, seen here approaching Dorridge.

Geoff Dowling

Plate 118: The failure of Class 56 No. 56001 at Hatton resulted in the unusual sight of Class 33 No. 33025 *Sultan* having charge of an empty merry-go-round rake from Didcot. The Class 33 had been borrowed from a Southampton-bound Freightliner train. *8th January 1983* *Geoff Dowling*

Plates 119 & 120: Twenty two years separate these two views which show the decline of the railway at Solihull. On 24th April 1963 Class 52 No. D1013 *Western Ranger* passes the extensive goods yard with the 15.10 Paddington to Wolverhampton (Low Level) working. By August 1985, the goods yard has been redeveloped and the station rationalised. Class 47 No. 47537 *Sir Gwynedd/County of Gwynedd* hauls the 13.40 (SO) Poole to Birmingham train.

Michael Mensing and Geoff Dowling

Plate 121: Heavy overnight snow has caused operational difficulties as Class 47 No. 47531, deputising for an HST, passes Lapworth Station with the 09.15 Bristol to Newcastle Sunday service on 10th February 1985.

Geoff Dowling

Plate 122: An interesting race from Solihull. Class 47 No. D1700, hauling the 07.55 Leamington Spa (General) to Birkenhead train, is leading BR Standard 2-6-4 tank No. 80072 which is heading the 07.45 Leamington to Birmingham (Snow Hill). A southbound diesel multiple unit completes the scene.

8th April 1964   *Michael Mensing*

STOP
AND AWAIT
INSTRUCTIONS
END OF OTO
LINE

Plate 123 (above): All that remains of the Honeybourne to Stratford-upon-Avon line is a truncated link to Long Marston Army Depot. Class 31 No. 31402 slowly clears the yard on the return journey to Worcester on 30th May 1985.

Geoff Dowling

Plate 124 (below): In 1969, Honeybourne Station was closed, and the buildings were demolished. One year earlier, Class 35 No. 7081 leads a Worcester-bound freight off the Stratford-upon-Avon line. The station reopened in 1981.

Ronald Swift

Plate 125 (above): Class 50 No. 50041 *Bulwark* approaches Evesham with the 16.30 Worcester (Shrub Hill) to Paddington service in May 1982, a few weeks before the 'Cotswold Line' lost most of its locomotive-hauled services. Happily, this trend is now being reversed.

John Whitehouse

Plate 126 (below): Evesham once had two stations, the Midland (which closed in 1963) and the GWR which still remains in good repair. On 25th July 1981, Class 50 No. 50004 *St. Vincent* draws to a halt with the 10.50 Paddington to Worcester (Shrub Hill) working.

Geoff Dowling

Plate 127: The sun breaks through to provide welcome illumination of the 10.39 Cardiff to Newcastle HST at Oddingley, near Droitwich, on 22nd October 1983. The fisherman remains impassive to the activity behind him.

Geoff Dowling

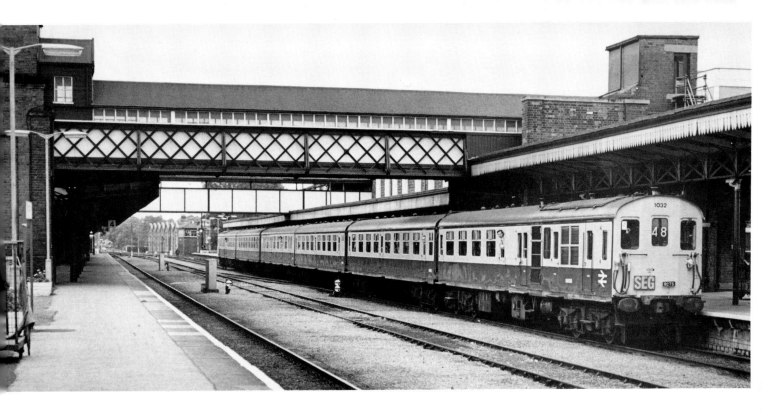

Plate 128: A stranger to Worcester, on 13th October 1984, was Class 202 diesel electric multiple unit forming a railtour from Hastings to Kidderminster (for the Severn Valley Railway).

Geoff Dowling

Plate 129: Class 45/1 No. 45127 approaches Oddingley crossing signal box with the 09.05 Plymouth to York service on 22nd October 1983.

Geoff Dowling

Plate 130: Blakedown seems to be tumbling down on this very wet evening in May 1976 as Class 52 No. 1013 *Western Ranger* heads for Kidderminster with the empty stock for a returning railtour that had visited the Severn Valley Railway.

Paul Townsend

Plate 131: Although the station shows signs of rationalisation, Hagley still has a magnificent ex-GWR footbridge which acts as a perfect frame for the 08.00 Bristol to Newcastle IC125 Sunday service. Note the ornate ironwork coat of arms and the date on the bridge.
23rd June 1985

Geoff Dowling

Plate 132: HST power car No. 43164 leads the 07.55 Plymouth to Newcastle train through Kidderminster Junction on 23rd June 1985. The junction is now with the Severn Valley Railway, whose tracks lead away on the right.
Geoff Dowling

Plate 133: Now enjoying a new lease of life in preservation on the Severn Valley Railway, Class 52 No. 1062 *Western Courier*, fresh from overhaul, contrasts sharply with the GWR-pattern steam locomotive boiler, as it leads a Bridgnorth to Kidderminster service from Bewdley.
7th October 1984
Geoff Dowling

Plate 134 (above): In the heart of the British Leyland complex at Longbridge, a Diesel Hydraulic shunting locomotive named *Frankley* deals with a raft of coal wagons. Note the ex-Midland Railway signal box. *2nd April 1984*   *Geoff Dowling.*

Plate 135 (left): The British Leyland factory forms the backdrop as Class 50 No. 50011 *Centurion* rushes by at the head of the 11.23 Manchester to Plymouth service on 20th April 1984.

Ivor Ford

Plate 136: Trains on the cross-country route via Birmingham have been associated with 'Peak' class loco-motives since the early days of dieselisation. Working hard on the southbound climb to Blackwell, an unidenti-fied member of the class sweeps through Barnt Green during the summer of 1977.

John Whitehouse

Plate 137: The Redditch branch leaves the main line at Barnt Green, where Class 101 unit No. 53310 leads a Redditch to Cam-bridge excursion cau-tiously through the tight curve on 28th April 1984.

Geoff Dowling

Plate 138 Although the station buildings at Alvechurch were demolished some years ago, the station house is still occupied and in good condition. A Class 116 unit, with 'customised' window surrounds, completes the scene with the 16.25 Redditch to Blake Street service.
13th July 1985   Geoff Dowling

Plate 139: An evening rush hour service from Lichfield, formed of the usual Class 116 unit, passes the outer home signal at Redditch.
5th May 1984   Geoff Dowling

Plate 140: Class 50 No. 50036 *Victorious*, having just climbed the Lickey Incline, heads towards Barnt Green with the 07.35 Plymouth to Birmingham working on 30th December 1983. Blackwell Hospital can be seen on the horizon above the locomotive.
Geoff Dowling

Plate 141: A snow-encrusted Class 47, No. 47534, reaches the Lickey Summit at Blackwell with the 09.34 Cardiff to Manchester train on 12th December 1981. Note the sudden change of gradient at this point.
Geoff Dowling

Plate 142: A late 1968 scene at Bromsgrove before the track realignments, which also saw the semaphore signalling replaced. An unidentified 'Warship' class diesel hydraulic awaits the road.

Ronald Swift

Plate 143: Ex-LMS 4-6-2 No. 6201 *Princess Elizabeth* is probably on its way to Tyseley for an open day as it is shepherded through Bromsgrove towards the Lickey Incline with Class 35 'Hymek' No. 7083 at the front, and two more at the rear. However, who is pushing and pulling who seems very much open to question.

circa 1970   Ronald Swift

Plate 144: Bromsgrove has always been known for its banking engines and, nowadays, two Class 37s fulfil this role. Nos. 37295 and 37129 await their next duty as Class 46 No. 46026 *Leicestershire and Derbyshire Yeomanry* speeds past with a Glasgow to Bristol relief.
28th April 1984   *Geoff Dowling*

Plate 145: Class 47 No. 47433 approaches Droitwich with a Llandudno to Worcester charter on 28th April 1984, having travelled via Bromsgrove. Leading away to the left is the line to Kidderminster.
                                                                                                                                        Geoff Dowling

Plate 146: The low winter sun picks out the trackwork of Worcester Tunnel Junction as Class 119 diesel multiple unit heads towards Droitwich with the 10.28 Hereford to Birmingham train on 8th December 1984. The 13th century cathedral stands proud in the morning mist.

Geoff Dowling

Plate 147: HSTs were introduced on to 'Cotswold Line' services in May 1984 and form an out and back working from Paddington, 'The Malvern Express'. The train is seen leaving Worcester (Foregate Street) Station. *10th December 1984*   *Geoff Dowling*

Plate 148 (above): A Class 119 diesel multiple unit approaches Worcester (Foregate Street) Station in June 1984 with a service from Hereford. Two-way working operates at this point.

John Whitehouse

Plate 149 (below): Class 50 No. 50027 *Lion* arrives at Great Malvern with the 16.10 Paddington to Hereford Sunday working.
7th July 1985   *Geoff Dowling*

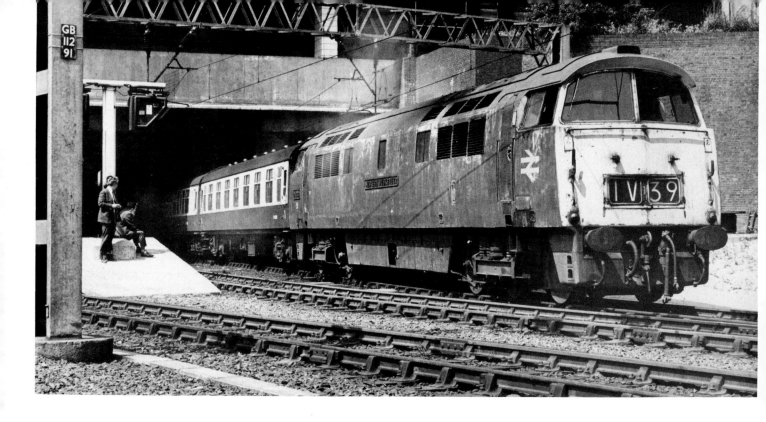

Plate 151 (below): Birmingham (New Street) Station at night, as Class 50 No. 50018 *Resolution* prepares for the last leg of its journey to Wolverhampton with the 17.40 service from Paddington.
19th December 1984

Geoff Dowling

Plate 150 (left): Emerging from the gloom of Birmingham (New Street), Class 52 No. D1030 *Western Musketeer* heads the 12.25 service to Paddington in June 1974.

John Whitehouse

Plates 152 (right) & 153 (below): Twenty five years span these photographs, yet the Class 101 units are still going strong. On 17th September 1960 (right) a member of the class forms the 16.20 Redditch service whilst 'Crab' 2-6-0 No. 42859 stands alongside. On 9th February 1985, with snow providing a curious eyebrow effect, a Class 101 multiple unit stands in Birmingham (New Street) forming empty stock for Wolverhampton. It will follow Class 86 electric locomotive No. 86219 *Phoenix*.

Michael Mensing and John Whitehouse

Plate 154: Birmingham (Moor Street) Station was built to ease pressure on Snow Hill and survives due to its suburban role. On 9th February 1985, a Class 116 diesel multiple unit departs with the late-running 13.10 service to Stratford-upon-Avon.

John Whitehouse

Plate 155: Old and new at Birmingham: the distinctive GWR design of the buildings at Birmingham (Moor Street) contrasts with the neon-crowned Rotunda edifice. Class 116 motor brake No. M51133 will form the 20.40 working to Shirley.
19th December 1984   *Geoff Dowling*

Plate 156: Nicknamed locally as 'The Ghost Train', the Wolverhampton (Low Level) to Birmingham service arrives at Birmingham (Snow Hill) formed of a Class 122 unit. The service survived until 1972.
circa 1969

John Vaughan

Plate 157: The Snow Hill that everyone remembers. The 14.30 Pullman service to Paddington awaits departure in the hands of a Metro-Cammell 'Blue Pullman' set on 23rd February 1961.

Michael Mensing

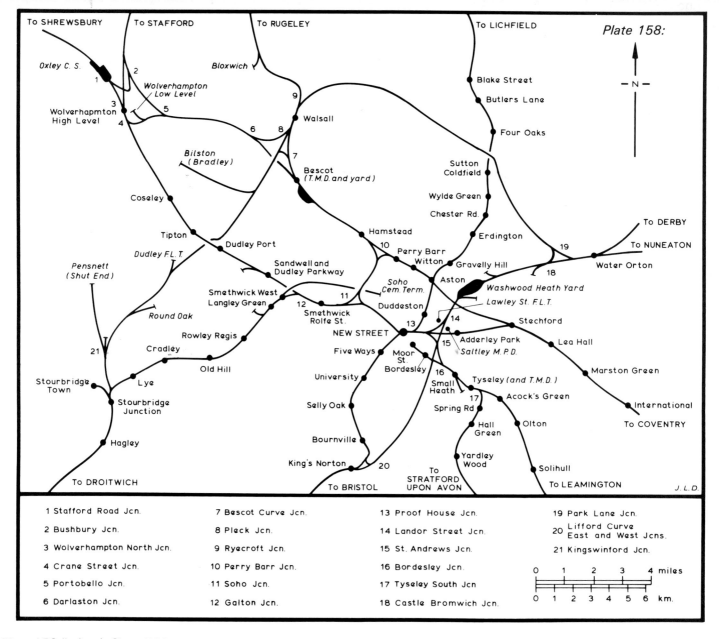

To SHREWSBURY · To STAFFORD · To RUGELEY · To LICHFIELD

Plate 158:

← N →

Oxley C. S.
1
2
Bloxwich
9
Blake Street
Butlers Lane
Four Oaks

Wolverhampton Low Level
3
5
Wolverhapmton High Level
4
Walsall
6
8

Bilston (Bradley)
7
Bescot (T.M.D. and yard)

Sutton Coldfield
Wylde Green
Chester Rd.

Coseley
Erdington
19

Tipton
Hamstead
10
Perry Barr
Witton
Gravelly Hill
Aston
18
To DERBY
To NUNEATON
Water Orton

Dudley F.L.T.
Pensnett (Shut End)
Dudley Port
Sandwell and Dudley Parkway
Soho Cem. Term.
Washwood Heath Yard
Lawley St. F.L.T.

Smethwick West
Langley Green
12
11
Duddeston
Stechford

Round Oak
Smethwick Rolfe St.
13
14

Rowley Regis
NEW STREET
15
Adderley Park
Saltley M.P.D.
Lea Hall

21
Cradley
Five Ways
Moor St.
Bordesley
Marston Green

Stourbridge Town
Lye
Old Hill
University
16
Small Heath
Tyseley (and T.M.D.)
International
To COVENTRY

Stourbridge Junction
Selly Oak
17
Spring Rd
Acock's Green
Olton

Hagley
Bournville
Hall Green
Yardley Wood
Solihull

King's Norton
20
To STRATFORD UPON AVON
To LEAMINGTON

To DROITWICH
To BRISTOL

J.L.D.

1 Stafford Road Jcn.	7 Bescot Curve Jcn.	13 Proof House Jcn.	19 Park Lane Jcn.
2 Bushbury Jcn.	8 Pleck Jcn.	14 Landor Street Jcn.	20 Lifford Curve East and West Jcns.
3 Wolverhampton North Jcn.	9 Ryecroft Jcn.	15 St. Andrews Jcn.	
4 Crane Street Jcn.	10 Perry Barr Jcn.	16 Bordesley Jcn.	21 Kingswinford Jcn.
5 Portobello Jcn.	11 Soho Jcn.	17 Tyseley South Jcn	
6 Darlaston Jcn.	12 Galton Jcn.	18 Castle Bromwich Jcn.	

0 1 2 3 4 miles
0 1 2 3 4 5 6 km.

Plate 159 (below): Class 50 No. 50034 *Furious* has the skyline of Birmingham as a background on 9th May 1982 at Exchange Sidings.

Geoff Dowling

Plate 160: Rounding Bordesley Junction is Class 31 No. 31170 with a Sunday Engineer's 'drain train' on 26th August 1985. Note the huge BR warehouse, in front of which runs the ex-GWR main line, now terminating at Birmingham (Moor Street).

John Whitehouse

Plate 161: Class 58 No. 58025 trips four 'cartic' wagons from Small Heath to Washwood Heath, through St. Andrews Junction on 16th July 1985.

Geoff Dowling

Plate 162 (above): An unidentified Class 47/4 emerges from the tunnelled exit from Birmingham (New Street) at Five Ways with the 09.22 Newcastle to Penzance train. The abandoned tunnel on the right once carried the line to the Midland goods depot at Suffolk Street.
26th June 1984
Geoff Dowling

Plate 163 (top right): A new face on test over the 'Cross-City' line. Class 143 unit No. 143001 is seen at Selly Oak on 20th September 1985 simulating normal operations.

Geoff Dowling

Plate 164 (bottom right): The temperature can be judged by the icicles hanging from the front of unit No. 53078, as it passes through Edgbaston Tunnel with a Longbridge to Four Oaks service on 9th February 1985.
Geoff Dowling

Plate 165: In the days before investment in the Cross City line, Selly Oak was virtually derelict, as this 1974 view illustrates. Class 31 No. 31291 heads towards Birmingham (New Street) with a northbound express.
Geoff Dowling

Plate 166: The Worcester Canal follows the line out of Birmingham for some distance, frequently side by side, as this view near Birmingham University shows. An ailing Class 50 No. 50017 struggles towards New Street with the 12.35 Worcester to Paddington service (via Birmingham).
6th March 1978
Geoff Dowling

Plate 167: Evaluation trials brought a Class 150 into revenue-earning service for one week in May 1985. Working the 11.16 Blake Street to Longbridge service, the unit skirts the Worcester Canal and approaches University Station on 11th May 1985.

Geoff Dowling

Plate 168: With the Camp Hill line divering on the right, Class 50 No. 50038 *Formidable* heads the 11.23 Manchester to Plymouth train through King's Norton on 28th April 1984.

Geoff Dowling

Plate 169 (above): Class 50 No. 50040 *Leviathan* bursts out of Moseley Tunnel on the Camp Hill line with the 08.53 Newquay to Manchester working on 22nd September 1984.

John Whitehouse

Plate 170 (top right): Class 47 No. 47119 passes the site of Hazelwell Station on the Camp Hill line. It was temporarily closed as an emergency measure in 1941, and shut totally in 1946. The train is bound for Long-bridge to collect scrap from Austin-Rover.
9th April 1984   *Geoff Dowling*

Plate 171 (bottom right): Super power for the Curzon Street to Worcester parcels in the form of Class 47 No. 47298. It is taking the Camp Hill line past the old King Edward's Grammar School building.
26th June 1984   *Geoff Dowling*

Plate 172: Most of the modern London underground stock was built by Metropolitan-Cammell at Washwood Heath. Providing an interesting comparison, Class 25 No. 25265 heads a train of new stock destined for Neasden.
15th June 1984 *Geoff Dowling*

Plate 173: Passing Saltley Trading Estate with the diverted 10.18 Birmingham to Euston working on 11th March 1984, is Class 47 No. 47551.
Geoff Dowling

Plate 174 (above): For a while, Saltley turned out a Class 50 on the 19.15 Lawley Street to Felixstowe Freightliner. The locomotive would work to Nuneaton and, on 13th May 1985, No. 50011 *Centurion* has charge of the train.

Geoff Dowling

Plate 175 (below): Lawley Street Freightliner Terminal on a wet November evening. Class 58 No. 58015 has the 20.15 to Felixstowe whilst Class 37 No. 37009 stands with the Avonmouth to Boulby Potash empties.

Geoff Dowling

Plate 176 (left): The tube works sidings of British Steel lie alongside the main Derby line at Bromford Bridge, and their shunter is working the yard on 12th August 1984. Dominating the background is the M6 motorway.

Geoff Dowling

Plate 177 (below): Washwood Heath Sidings hosts Class 37 No. 37172 at the head of a train load of scrap metal. The locomotive would appear to be a recent transfer from Scotland, judging by the 'Highland Terrier' motif of Eastfield Depot on the side.
9th March
1985   *Geoff Dowling*

Plate 178: Passing Washwood Heath Sidings No. 1 signal box, Class 47 No. 47281 heads the 12.35 from Yarmouth towards Birmingham (New Street) on 3rd August 1985. The Aston to Stechford line crosses the Midland route at this point and can be seen behind the train.

Geoff Dowling

Plate 179: Castle Bromwich Station closed in 1967, but the remains of the 'up' platform are still visible as Class 45/1 No. 45126 passes at the head of a Birmingham to Leicester Footex, on 27th October 1984.

Robin Banks

Plate 180: The line to Stourbridge, via Cradley Heath, is being developed as another 'Cross-City' route and, eventually, it will join the Solihull line via the reopened Birmingham (Snow Hill) Tunnel and Station. The 16.15 Birmingham to Worcester train draws into Lye, one of several local stations on the line.
18th June 1983   Geoff Dowling

Plate 181: The substantial station buildings at Rowley Regis dwarf Class 45/0 No. 45044, running light engine from Stourbridge where it would have performed banking duties.
24th March 1982   Geoff Dowling

Plate 182: The branch to Stour-bridge Town enjoys a frequent service operated by a Class 122 unit. On 30th December 1983, car No. M55012 unloads at the new Town Station. The site of the old station is now the bus interchange point at the rear.

Geoff Dowling

Plate 183: A Class 47, No. 47129, heads through Langley Green with a rake of tanks on 8th June 1984. The remains of the Oldbury branch leads off to the right. Note the splendid lower quadrant semaphores.

Geoff Dowling

Plates 184 & 185: On 30th May 1965, Class 47 No. D1746 passes Handsworth and Smethwick Station with the 09.25 Paddington to Chester service. The station closed in 1972, but the remains can be seen as Class 25 No. 25283 works the 16.15 trip from Soho Cement Terminal in 1985.

Michael Mensing and Geoff Dowling

Plate 186: On 5th June 1985 near the old Hawthorns Halt, Class 31 No. 31127 works a trip from Langley Green to the cement terminal at Soho.

Geoff Dowling

Plate 187: Some twenty years earlier, Class 40s Nos. D214 *Antonia* and D304 pass Hawthorns Halt with the diverted 12.10 Birmingham to Blackpool train. The ex-GWR route saw renewed activity while the neighbouring Stour Valley and Grand Junction lines were electrified.

Michael Mensing

Plate 188: Oldbury Station was extended on the parkway principle and renamed Sandwell and Dudley in May 1984. On 10th August 1985, Class 45/0 No. 45070 calls with the 12.38 Llandudno to Birmingham service.
John Whitehouse

Plate 189: At Winson Green, the foreground piers once carried the Harborne branch, which closed to passengers in 1934, and totally in 1963. On the main line, passing under the Dudley Road is Class 31 No. 31422 with the stock for the 15.25 Birmingham to Cambridge service on 25th April 1984.
Geoff Dowling

Plates 190 & 191: A Rugeley-bound diesel multiple unit takes the Walsall line at Bescot on 17th March 1962. The scene is now totally changed; not only has electrification arrived, but also the M6 motorway. Class 47 No. 47549 leads the diverted 13.05 Birmingham to Liverpool Sunday service towards Walsall.

4th September 1983   *Michael Mensing and John Whitehouse*

Plate 192: A Class 116 diesel multiple unit pauses at Aston with an early evening Lichfield to Longbridge service. Note the junction with the avoiding line to Stechford.
19th August 1985   *John Whitehouse*

Plate 193: A Sunday diversion via Cannock Chase bring the 09.00 Plymouth to Manchester HST working and Class 47 No. 47524 with the 10.24 Liverpool to Birmingham to Pleck Junction, Walsall, on 17th March 1985.
                                                                                                            John Whitehouse

Plate 194: A major event was the opening in 1976 of Birmingham International Station to serve the National Exhibition Centre. Later, a link via the 'Maglev' was made with the new Birmingham Airport Terminal building. On 27th July 1985, Class 47 No. 47329 passes with a Coatbridge to Southampton Freightliner train.
Geoff Dowling

Plate 195: The arrival of the Motor Show at the National Exhibition Centre attracts many extra trains. To avoid congestion in Birmingham (New Street), many run via the Aston to Stechford line. A returning special to Manchester approaches Aston on 27th October 1984, behind Class 47 No. 47446.
Geoff Dowling

Plate 196: Adderley Park Yard is now virtually disused, but in happier days, May 1981, Class 25 No. 25195 performs shunting duties.

Geoff Dowling

Plate 197: Adderley Park is the first station from Birmingham (New Street) on the Coventry line. On a summer Saturday in 1983, Class 50 No. 50018 *Resolution* passes at the head of the 13.07 from Paddington, whilst a local service, consisting of a Class 312 electric multiple unit, pauses in the station.

John Whitehouse

Plate 198: Stechford shunt frame signal box is visible on the left as a Class 47 sweeps through heading the 05.50 Paddington to Manchester service. The line from Aston converges from the left.

John Whitehouse

Plate 199: Class 50 No. 50046 *Ajax* is about to cross the River Blythe at Hampton-in-Arden, whilst working the 14.38 Birmingham to Paddington service on 23rd January 1982.

Geoff Dowling

Plate 200: Class 44 'Peaks' regularly worked into Bescot on the daily freight from Toton. In September 1977, No. 44004, with nameplate *Great Gable* removed, heads through Walsall with a northbound van train.

John Whitehouse

Plate 201: Class 45/0 No. 45022 leads the Bescot to Toton freight over Rushall Crossing on 9th March 1984, some ten days before the line closed.

Geoff Dowling

Plate 202: The ex-GWR branch from Langley Green to Oldbury is retained as far as the Albright & Wilson chemical works. A daily trip uses the branch, and Class 31 No. 31163 can be seen propelling the tanks towards Langley Green *(see Plate 183)*.
15th November 1983   Geoff Dowling

Plate 203: Class 08 shunter No. 08590 trips a short freight from Norton Junction (near Brownhills) to Bescot. It is seen between Ryecroft Junction and Walsall in June 1977.

John Whitehouse

Plate 204: On 2nd June 1977, Class 25 No. 25038 heads away from Wednesbury towards Dudley with a short pick-up freight. It has just passed under the closed ex-GWR main line from Birmingham to Wolverhampton, which was being used as a siding. Now the line has been lifted and the bridge demolished.
Robin Banks

Plate 205: Dudley Freightliner Terminal, with Class 37 No. 37087 and the 18.45 Dudley to Glasgow Freightliner train. This is the site of Dudley Station, which closed in 1964.
30th May 1985
Geoff Dowling

Plate 206: Class 47 No. 47061 shunts the LCP Fuels plant at Pensnett, which is the present terminus of the former Kingswinford Junction to Oxley branch.
8th May 1985   *Geoff Dowling*

Plate 207: High above the Dudley Canal at Netherton, Class 31 No. 31296 heads the 12.45 Bescot to Severn Tunnel Junction freight on 23rd November 1983.

Geoff Dowling

Plate 208: Tyseley Diesel Depot by night.
23rd March 1981

Ivor Ford

Plate 209: Saltley by night.
19th August 1985

Geoff Dowling